The Li

GW00514813

Hugs & Kisses

by Charlie Watson
Illustrations by Richard Lowdell

Nightingale
An imprint of Wimbledon Publishing Company
LONDON

Copyright © 2000
Illustrations © 2000 WPC

First published in Great Britain in 2000
by Wimbledon Publishing Company Ltd
P.O. Box 9779 London SW19 7ZG
All rights reserved

First published 2000 in Great Britain

ISBN: 1903222 11 7

Produced in Great Britain
Printed and bound in Hungary

Hugs

and Kisses

A hug and a kiss - two of the best ways to show you care - in theory. Much of the time, however, these romantic gestures don't quite live up to our expectations, and a fabulous session of tonsil tennis is easily marred by bad breath or excessive dribble.

These poems provide a roundup of classic intimate scenarios. If you're lucky, you'll have found yourself in most of these predicaments at one time or another. Hopefully, these poems will remind you of clumsy fumbles and secretive slobbers.

Or course, if you think they're best avoided in the future, just remember that practice makes perfect.
Happy kissing!

Charlie Watson
1999

The First Kiss

Do you remember long ago
When I came round for tea?
I made a move to hold your hand
Whilst watching your T.V.
You were my first, you felt so sweet
Your lips relayed love's laws
We kissed for hours until I cramped,
It broke my heart to pause.

A Gran's Kiss

If only my Gran were less forward
And greeted me not with a kiss,
She lost all her teeth in the Fifties
And kisses just like a wet fish.

The Hairy Kiss

A kiss with a man is a curious thing
When shaven his stubble will scratch,
And any girl dating a man with a beard
Must bury her face in his thatch.

The Toothy Kiss

Her teeth are white, but maybe too bold
And therefore her lips can't conceal,
Enamel protrusions that jut from her mouth
And give her that 'Stone Henge' appeal.
Her kiss is both pleasure and anguish
A flirt with enamel and lip,
The latter seducing me softly
Before the teeth give me a nip.

The Wet Kiss

It started out drily, a cautious approach
Her warm lips enfolding me in,
We kissed for a while then I took a breather
To wipe all her drool off my chin.

The Continental Kiss

A kiss on each cheek provides double the fun
A sensual exchange when you meet,
From babies and children to ladies and gents
It's surely the best way to greet.
But some of the city girls ruin the moment
And say it's passé to draw near,
Modern trends show that disinterest is cool
So they kiss several feet from each ear.

The French Kiss

I can't believe that the French could have started
The fashion of kissing with tongues,
It strikes me as odd that a nation of chefs
Could forage for food in strange gums.

The Peck

Of all the kisses, the peck is the worst
'Tis rarely emotionally planted,
It's often a signal your love's not returned
Or feelings are taken for granted.
For all the affection you show on a date
It's cruel when your charm is forgotten,
The silly young lady deciding to pucker
Instead of just snogging you rotten.

The Maul

You'll always find out by the time it's too late
If romance is one of his skills,
Or if he thinks love is an animal trait
And snogs like a predator kills.
'Coz as you prepare for the sweetness to come
The beast could be gnashing his jaws,
Preparing to jump at your innocent mouth
And stifle your protests with roars.

The Baby's Kiss

A baby's lack of control in the kiss
Can cause considerable laughter,
On planting their lips they pull right away
And smack their lips five seconds after.

A Blown Kiss

On having to leave me at nursery school
My Mum used to blow me a kiss,
And I would leap wildly around in the air
For fear the affection might miss.

The Elderly Kiss

We oldies are proof that love's deeper
Than glamour or physical whim,
Its beauty refuses to wither
Its strength doesn't fade with our skin.
And so when I'm kissing my Edna
I know what love's truly about,
Ignoring her copious wrinkles
And false teeth which keep falling out.

The Manly Hug

When men need to bond with each other
Their wild fervour reaching a high,
Then fall the fetters of sexual restraint
And so they'll embrace any guy.
But just to avoid the perception
They're acting in womanly fashion,
They'll beat their mate hard on the shoulder
To take the heat out of their passion.

The Gentleman's Embrace

For gentlemen nothing's more awkward

Than when manners force an embrace,

Propriety usually calls for restraint

And restraint is the way to save face,

But if a companion had done something rash

And risked his health saving your life,

You'd just have to hug him,

Say, 'Thank you, dear boy,'

Then, 'Steady, you know I've a wife!'

The Lover's Hug

Our bodies fit better and closer
Now that we've loved for some years
My chin rests content on your shoulder
Your cheek warms the side of my ear,
My chest moves in time with your breathing
My heart matches yours pound for pound,
The only dilemma - I'm not very tall
And you're holding me way off the ground.

The Mother's Embrace

My Mum used to give me such comfort
Whenever I'd fallen from grace,
And when I'd been outcast or bullied
She'd fling wide her arms and embrace.
At first her hugs made me feel stronger
At times when I thought myself weak,
But often the way that she smothered
Would leave me unable to speak.

The Unwanted Hug

A pleasant thing in gross excess
Can make one feel quite nauseous,
A hug is one such show of love
With which one must be cautious.
It is the over-zealous types
With whom I find the fault,
Whose tawdry hugs for hugging's sake
Amount to gross assault.

The Stiff Hug

Whenever I'm hugging my boyfriend
In public where others can see.
He tenses and tries to look macho
It's just like I'm dating a tree.

The Sicilian Embrace

The Godfather greeting his henchmen
Will offer the warmest of hugs,
Convincing each one that he's vital
To swindle and thieve and run drugs.
'You're key to the family business
We honour the love that you give.'
However, the longer he clinches
The less time he'll give you to live.

The Toddler's Hug

When I am older and grown up a bit
I plan to hug Dad round the waist,
Because when you're three
and you try to show love,
You get knobbled knees in the face.

The Judas Kiss

Whilst drinking a pint down Gethsemane Arms

A man I knew stepped to the bar,

'Twas Jeremy Jude, with a strange-looking bloke

Who held in his hand a silk bra.

Approaching me smiling, Jez gave me a kiss

Which gave me the fright of my life,

At which point the man with the underwear screamed,

So it's you who's had sex with my wife!'

The Halitosis Kiss

You kiss me quite nicely, the feeling is soft

Your lips form a good enough pout,

Just one thing I fear are the fumes from your mouth

And the smell of dead fish seeping out.

The Wedding Kiss

I heard the priest say, 'You may now kiss the bride'

And I sensually pulled up her veil

I lowered my head to the love of my life

And set our new love out to sail.

But as I was snogging a hideous thought

Some horror careered through my mind

I wondered what pleasure those very same lips

Would give me in sixty years time.

The Bear Hug

At 21 stones I may look like an ogre
But still I need kisses and hugs,
Sadly my friends seem to break when I squeeze
And those that don't think I'm a thug.

The Farewell Kiss

The final kiss you gave me
Was torture to my soul
The last touch of your ruby lips
Inspired this empty hole
That bores into my lover's heart
And makes me feel the fool,
What fate provoked your progress
From here to junior school?

The Film Kiss

I learnt all my skills from the movies
And studied the lips of Tom Cruise,
I felt if I mimicked his passion
No woman alive could refuse.
Sadly on snogging some filly
I found myself stuck in a rut,
The lighting was wrong,
The girls used her tongue,
And no one was there to scream, 'Cut!'

The Forgiving Hug

When you're feeling moody
And 'sorry' just won't work,
There's nothing like a warm embrace
To show you've been a jerk.

The Lecherous Uncle

I have a strange and aged uncle
comes at Christmas time,
He spends the festive season
Paralytic on mulled wine,
Until beneath the mistletoe
His seasonal behest,
He'll ask me for a friendly kiss
And try to squeeze me breast.

Bye!